TEAM SPIRIT®

SMART BOOKS FOR YOUNG FANS

THE NEW JERSEY DEVILS

BY

MARK STEWART

CONTENT CONSULTANT
DENIS GIBBONS
SOCIETY FOR INTERNATIONAL HOCKEY RESEARCH

NORWOOD HOUSE PRESS

CHICAGO, ILLINOIS

Norwood House Press
P.O. Box 316598
Chicago, Illinois 60631

For information regarding Norwood House Press, please visit our website at:
www.norwoodhousepress.com or call 866-565-2900.

All photos courtesy of Associated Press except the following:
Topps, Inc. (6, 7, 15, 21, 34 right, 37, 38, 39, 42 top),
Getty Images (8, 10, 11, 12, 22, 25, 27, 28, 31, 34 top left), The National Hockey League (9, 40),
Beckett Publications (17, 45), Fleer Corp. (22), O-Pee-Chee Ltd. (23, 35 top right, 42 bottom),
The New Jersey Devils (33, 41), Author's Collection (34 left),
Hockey Hall of Fame (38), Black Book Partners (43 top).
Cover Photo: Cal Sport Media via AP Images

The memorabilia and artifacts pictured in this book are presented for educational and informational purposes,
and come from the collection of the author.

Editor: Mike Kennedy
Designer: Ron Jaffe
Project Management: Black Book Partners, LLC.
Special thanks to Topps, Inc.

Library of Congress Cataloging-in-Publication Data

Stewart, Mark, 1960 July 7-
  The New Jersey Devils / by Mark Stewart. -- Revised edition.
     pages cm. -- (Team spirit)
  Includes bibliographical references and index.
  Summary: "A revised Team Spirit Hockey edition featuring the New Jersey
Devils that chronicles the history and accomplishments of the team. Includes
access to the Team Spirit website which provides additional information and
photos"-- Provided by publisher.
  ISBN 978-1-59953-623-1 (library edition : alk. paper) -- ISBN
978-1-60357-631-4 (ebook) 1. New Jersey Devils (Hockey
team)--History--Juvenile literature. 2. Hockey teams--United
States--Juvenile literature. I. Title.
  GV848.N38S74 2014
  796.962'640974932--dc23
                                                        2013034578

Manufactured in the United States of America in Stevens Point, Wisconsin.
239N—012014

COVER PHOTO: The Devils are never short on team spirit, especially after scoring a goal.

TABLE OF CONTENTS

ABOUT OUR GLOSSARY

In this book, there may be several words that you are reading for the first time. Some are sports words, some are new vocabulary words, and some are familiar words that are used in an unusual way. All of these words are defined on page 46. Throughout the book, sports words appear in **bold type**. Regular vocabulary words appear in *bold italic type*.

MEET THE DEVILS

Which is more frightening, the legendary creature known as the New Jersey Devil *or* a player for the New Jersey Devils? The first is a myth, but not the second. The Devils are a very real team—and very frightening, if you happen to be wearing a different color uniform.

The Devils do things a little differently than other teams in the **National Hockey League (NHL)**. From their coach to their top scorers to the last man on the bench, they work extra-hard to blend their strengths in ways that make them difficult to beat. There are no superstars on the team. Night in and night out, everyone plays as if their jobs depend on it.

This book tells the story of the Devils. After years of struggle and uncertainty, they discovered the key to championship hockey. Along the way, the team made stops in two other cities. But once the Devils arrived in New Jersey, they finally felt right at home.

David Clarkson, Patrik Elias, and Mattias Tedenby jump for joy after a big goal during the 2012–13 season.

GLORY DAYS

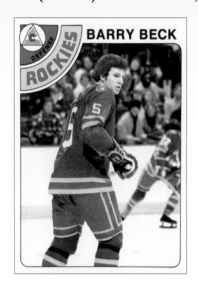

BARRY BECK

oes every big city in North America deserve its own **professional** hockey team? In the 1960s and 1970s, people sure seemed to think that way. The NHL expanded from six teams to 18. A new league called the **World Hockey Association (WHA)** also started, adding 12 more teams to the sport. One of the new NHL clubs arrived in Kansas City, Missouri, in 1974. After considering several names, the owners settled on Scouts, after a famous statue in Kansas City.

The Scouts would one day become the New Jersey Devils. Before moving east, however, the team actually headed west first. After two seasons, a mere 27 victories, and a lot of empty seats, the owners of the Scouts sold the club to a new group of owners in Denver, Colorado. It was the first time in more than 40 years that an NHL team switched cities.

The team was renamed the Rockies for the 1976–77 season. The club tried to draw fans with the promise of rough play. Many of

Colorado's best players—including Wilf Paiement, Barry Beck, Lanny McDonald, and Chico Resch—were physical and fearless leaders. Unfortunately, the team had trouble finding a winning *formula*, and the losing continued. The Rockies played for six seasons in Colorado without a winning record.

In 1982, a businessman named John McMullen bought the Rockies and moved the team to his home state of New Jersey. The club was renamed the Devils. New Jersey rebuilt around hardworking young players, including Kirk Muller, John MacLean, Pat Verbeek, Brendan Shanahan, Bruce Driver, and Sean Burke. In 1987–88, the Devils made the **playoffs** for the first time, and then nearly reached the **Stanley Cup Finals**. This unexpected success helped the team win over New Jersey sports fans. It also sparked a hockey craze among boys and girls across the state. Once-empty ice rinks were soon busy from morning to night.

Over the next 15 seasons, the Devils won the Stanley Cup three times. They were champions of the NHL in 1995, 2000, and 2003. The key to their success was a defensive style that slowed down

LEFT: Barry Beck starred for the team during its days in Colorado.
ABOVE: Kirk Muller helped hockey gain popularity in New Jersey.

opponents at center ice before they could organize their offensive attack. The Devils would wait patiently for the other team to become frustrated and make a mistake. Then they would steal the puck and score!

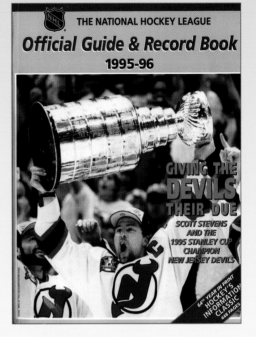

Because New Jersey concentrated on defense, many of the team's victories came in very close games. Often the difference was goaltending. This was where the Devils were strongest. Goalie Martin Brodeur was "between the pipes" for all three Stanley Cup championships. The bigger the game, the better Brodeur played. But he did more than make great saves. Often, he also triggered the offense by skating out of his net and sending the puck to his teammates. Brodeur was so good at this that the NHL actually made a new rule to limit how far from the **crease** that goalies could handle the puck.

New Jersey did not stock its **roster** with superstars. Instead, the Devils found smart, unselfish skaters who understood the importance of playing as a team. The club's scoring leaders included forwards Claude Lemieux, Patrik Elias, Bobby Holik, Jason Arnott, Petr Sykora, Sergei Brylin, Jamie Langenbrunner, Jay Pandolfo, and Scott Gomez. The defense was led by Scott Stevens,

LEFT: Martin Brodeur's great goaltending gave the Devils a huge advantage over opponents.   **ABOVE**: Scott Stevens lifts the Stanley Cup on the cover of the 1995–96 NHL Guide.

Scott Niedermayer, Brian Rafalski, and Ken Daneyko.

The only thing harder than winning a Stanley Cup is following up with another championship. The Devils showed they could do this by capturing the title three times in nine seasons. With each Stanley Cup, they learned a little more about what it takes to be the best. At the same time, other NHL clubs learned more about the New Jersey style of play. After their 2003 title, the Devils continued to improve by building on their championship experience and mixing young talent with trusted **veterans**.

Throughout this *era*, Brodeur continued to shine. In fact, he would go on to break almost every NHL goaltending record. Brodeur became the most famous player in team history and led the Devils through the first *decade* of the 21st *century*.

In the years that followed their Stanley Cup triumphs, the Devils learned just how hard it was to continue winning championships. The younger players on those championship teams matured into veteran leaders. Brodeur and Elias tutored newcomers such as Zach Parise, Ilya Kovalchuk, Adam Henrique, David Clarkson, and

Travis Zajac. They knew exactly what was expected of them when they joined the team.

Finally, in 2011–12, the Devils made their way back to the Stanley Cup Finals. They played defense like the Devils of old, with a little added scoring punch. And, of course, Brodeur was still in goal—for his 19th season! After surviving tough series against the Florida Panthers, Philadelphia Flyers, and **arch-rival** New York Rangers, Brodeur and the Devils fell two victories short of a fourth Stanley Cup. Although disappointed, their fans were glad that the winning formula still worked—and that they were still a super team, not a team of superstars.

LEFT: Claude Lemieux was a star for the Devils during their first Stanley Cup run.   **ABOVE**: Travis Zajac, Ilya Kovalchuk, and Zach Parise can't contain their excitement after a goal.

HOME ICE

For most of their history, the Devils shared their arena with the New Jersey Nets basketball team. It was part of the Meadowlands Sports Complex. The Devils moved to a beautiful new arena in downtown Newark for the 2007–08 season. In 2012, the Nets moved to Brooklyn, New York—leaving the Devils as the only **major-league** sports team that officially represents New Jersey.

Devils fans like to call their arena "The Rock" for the company that helped build it. New Jersey's arena has several high-definition (HD) video screens and scoreboards. It also has a mural that celebrates great moments in New Jersey sports. Martin Brodeur, Scott Stevens, and Ken Daneyko are among the athletes pictured.

BY THE NUMBERS

- The team's arena has 17,625 seats for hockey.
- There are 76 luxury suites in the arena.
- As of 2013–14, the Devils had retired three numbers: 3 (Ken Daneyko), 4 (Scott Stevens), and 27 (Scott Niedermayer).

Banners celebrating the Devils' achievements hang from the ceiling of the team's arena.

When the team played in Kansas City and Colorado, its main uniform color was blue. The Scouts *logo* showed a Native American on a horse. The Rockies logo was a mountain surrounding the letter *C*. After their move to New Jersey, the Devils switched their main colors to red and green. Their new logo had an *N* and *J* with a devil's horns and tail. In 1992–93, the team started using black instead of green.

WILF PAIEMENT • R.WING

Before the Devils ever played a game, some fans complained that the team was named after an evil being. The club met with religious leaders to make sure the name would not be a problem. Everyone agreed that the meaning of "devil" was clear—it was a make-believe monster that was said to live in the New Jersey Pine Barrens, and nothing more.

LEFT: Bryce Salvador wears the team's home uniform during a 2012–13 game.   **ABOVE**: This trading card features Wilf Paiement in the uniform of the Scouts.

WE WON!

After moving from Colorado to New Jersey, the Devils *labored* for five years without a winning record. Their luck finally changed in 1987–88, when they went 38–36–6 and made the playoffs for the first time. It took a goal in **overtime** by John MacLean in the final game of the regular season to grab the last playoff spot in the Eastern **Conference**.

In two exciting series, the Devils beat the New York Islanders and the Washington Capitals to reach the Eastern Conference Finals. New Jersey finally met its match in the Boston Bruins, who took the series in seven games. From that day forward, Devils fans would not settle for anything less than a trip to the Stanley Cup Finals.

They got their wish seven years later, when coach Jacques Lemaire made important changes to the club. Lemaire taught his players a defensive system called the "neutral zone trap." This move surprised many people—as a player, Lemaire was mostly known for his offensive skills. Meanwhile, he used four lines of forwards instead of three to keep his players from tiring out.

Martin Brodeur and the Devils proved the critics wrong in 1995.

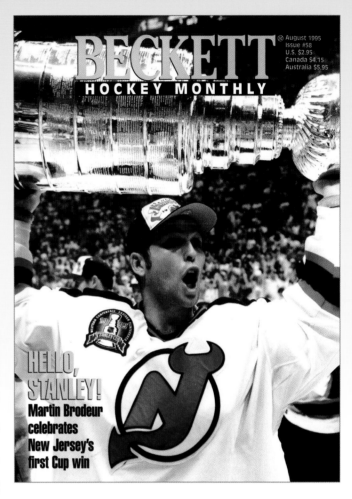

The Devils made the playoffs in 1994–95, but no one expected much of them. The Devils had won only eight games on the road that season. But once the playoffs started, they were sensational. The Devils lost only once as the visiting team in their run to the Stanley Cup Finals. Even so, most fans expected the Detroit Red Wings to wipe them out. "I'll never forget," says Randy McKay. "Four of the five papers were picking us to lose four straight."

Just the opposite happened. The Devils swept Detroit in four games. Everyone in the lineup chipped in. Neal Broten, who wasn't even on the team when the season started, scored the winning goal in Game 3 and then again in Game 4. Martin Brodeur

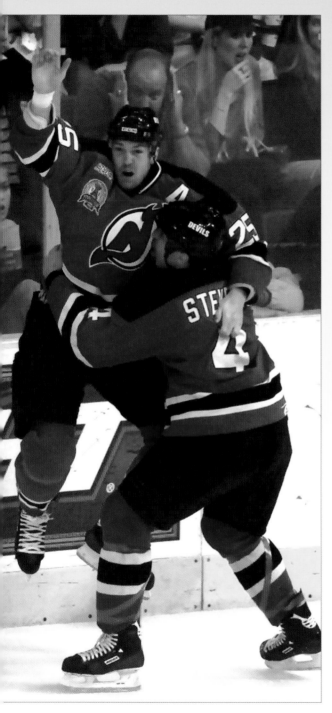

was sensational throughout the playoffs. He allowed less than two goals a game and recorded three **shutouts**. Claude Lemieux was just as good. In fact, he earned the Conn Smythe Trophy as the **Most Valuable Player (MVP)** of the playoffs. Lemieux scored 13 goals during the **postseason**.

The Devils won their second Stanley Cup in 2000. Again, people expected little from the team. With eight games left in the regular season, New Jersey replaced coach Robbie Ftorek with Larry Robinson. Normally, this is not a good sign. But the players stuck together and beat three good teams to reach the Stanley Cup Finals. There they faced the Dallas Stars, who had won the championship the year before.

Scott Stevens and Brodeur starred for the Devils. The last two games of the series were thrilling. The Stars won Game 5 in triple-overtime. The Devils bounced back two nights later to win in double-overtime. Jason Arnott scored the game-winning goal, as New Jersey celebrated its second championship.

New Jersey's third Stanley Cup came three years later. This time, expectations were very high. But the Devils were up to the challenge.

Their opponent in the Stanley Cup Finals was the Anaheim Ducks. The thrilling series went the full seven games. Brodeur recorded three shutouts, while Stevens and Scott Niedermayer played brilliant defense. As usual, everyone on the team contributed, including left wing Jeff Friesen, who scored five goals in the finals. It was a very satisfying feeling for Friesen. Before the season, Friesen had spent the past two years as a member of the Ducks!

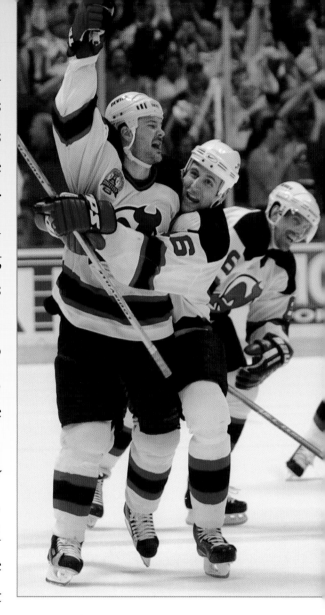

LEFT: Jason Arnott gets a big hug from Scott Stevens after his goal that won the 2000 Stanley Cup.   **ABOVE**: Jeff Friesen and Mike Rupp celebrate New Jersey's third championship.

GO-TO GUYS

To be a true star in the NHL, you need more than a great slapshot. You have to be a "go-to guy"—someone teammates trust to make the winning play when the seconds are ticking away in a big game. Fans of the Scouts, Rockies, and Devils have had a lot to cheer about over the years, including these great stars …

THE PIONEERS

WILF PAIEMENT   Right Wing

• Born: 10/16/1955   • Played for Team: 1974–75 to 1979–80

Wilf Paiement was the second pick in the 1974 NHL **draft**. He was a rough player with a hard, accurate shot. The result was a lot of goals—and a lot of time in the penalty box!

AARON BROTEN   Left Wing

• Born: 11/14/1960   • Played for Team: 1980–81 to 1989–90

Aaron Broten was drafted by the Rockies and became a star for the Devils. He could play center or wing and was as good as a **penalty-killer** as he was on the **power play**. His brother, Neal, played for the Devils in the 1990s.

RIGHT: John MacLean

JOHN MacLEAN   Right Wing

- BORN: 11/20/1964
- PLAYED FOR TEAM: 1983–84 TO 1997–98

John MacLean scored more than 40 goals three seasons in a row for New Jersey. MacLean was known as a *clutch* player. His overtime goal at the end of the 1987–88 season sent the Devils to the playoffs for the first time.

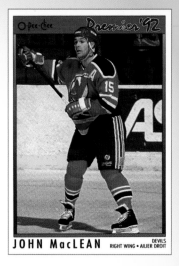

KEN DANEYKO   Defenseman

- BORN: 4/17/1964   • PLAYED FOR TEAM: 1983–84 TO 2002–03

Ken Daneyko was a "stay-at-home" defenseman. He was always in position to protect his net and didn't fire many shots against the opposing goalie. Daneyko spent all 20 of his NHL seasons with the Devils.

KIRK MULLER   Left Wing/Center

- BORN: 2/8/1966   • PLAYED FOR TEAM: 1984–85 TO 1990–91

The heart of the Devils during the 1980s was Kirk Muller. He played hard at both ends of the ice. In 1988, Muller led New Jersey to within one game of the Stanley Cup Finals.

SCOTT STEVENS   Defenseman

- BORN: 4/1/1964   • PLAYED FOR TEAM: 1991–92 TO 2003–04

Scott Stevens was a human wrecking ball. He used his size and speed to deliver crunching **checks**. Most of all, Stevens was a winner. When he retired, he had played in more regular-season victories (879) than any player in history.

MARTIN BRODEUR   Goalie

- BORN: 5/6/1972   • FIRST SEASON WITH TEAM: 1991–92

Few goalies have been as good for as long as Martin Brodeur. He set NHL career marks for wins, shutouts, and games played by a goalie. In 2009–10, he led the league in wins for the ninth time.

SCOTT NIEDERMAYER   Defenseman

- BORN: 8/31/1973   • PLAYED FOR TEAM: 1991–92 TO 2003–04

Scott Niedermayer played great defense and was a leader on the power play for the Devils. In 2003–04, the team allowed just two goals per game. After the season, Niedermayer won the Norris Trophy as the NHL's top defenseman.

BOBBY HOLIK   Center

- BORN: 4/13/1976
- PLAYED FOR TEAM: 1992–93 TO 2001–02 & 2008–09

Bobby Holik always demanded the best from himself and his teammates. No one on the team played harder or wanted to win more. Holik was a good scorer who never backed down from an opponent.

PATRIK ELIAS — Left Wing

- BORN 4/13/1976
- FIRST SEASON WITH TEAM: 1995–96

Most scorers have a favorite spot to shoot from. Patrik Elias could fire the puck from anywhere on the ice and find the back of the net. Elias set team records for goals and points (goals plus **assists**) in a career. He scored more than 70 game-winning goals as a Devil.

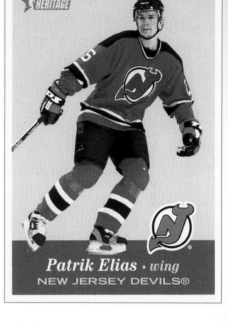

ZACH PARISE — Left Wing

- BORN: 7/28/1984
- PLAYED FOR TEAM: 2005–06 TO 2011–12

Zach Parise learned to play hockey from his father J.P., who appeared in the NHL **All-Star Game** twice. Parise was a good student. He had five 30-goal seasons for the Devils and was the hero for Team USA in the 2010 Winter *Olympics*.

DAVID CLARKSON — Right Wing

- BORN: 3/31/1984   • PLAYED FOR TEAM: 2006–07 TO 2012–13

When David Clarkson joined the Devils, he earned playing time with his hustle and hard-hitting style. By 2011–12, he had become one of their top goal-scorers—and one of the finest all-around players in the NHL.

LEFT: Bobby Holik
ABOVE: Patrick Elias

CALLING THE SHOTS

No coach in the NHL can truly say that his job is safe. When you coach for the Devils, that is especially true. The team hires coaches based on their ability to get the most out of the players on the roster. Winning isn't always enough. If the Devils believe another coach can do a better job, they will make a change at any time. So why do coaches want to work for the Devils? Because the team also gives them a lot of freedom.

Since 1987, the man who has had the most say in picking a coach for the Devils has been Lou Lamoriello. When he took control of the team, he had no experience in the NHL. Lamoriello knew college hockey inside-out, though. So he understood how to assemble and run a hockey team.

The Devils became winners almost every year under Lamoriello. He always tried to find a coach whose style matched the talent in the lineup. Jim Schoenfeld, Robbie Ftorek, Pat Burns, Larry Robinson, and Peter DeBoer all had different approaches to the game. Each had success coaching the Devils, but all of them were

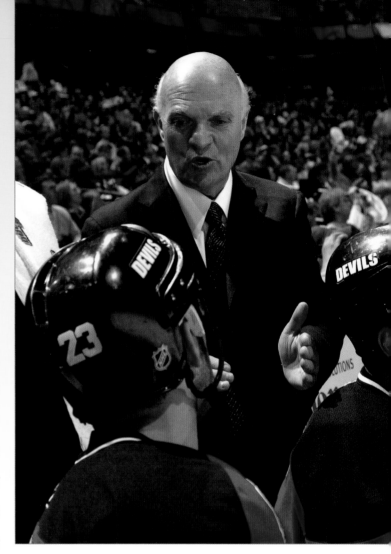

Lou Lamoriello was a coach for the Devils, but his greatest contributions came from running the team off the ice.

fired, too. When Lamoriello could not find the leader he wanted, he coached the team himself!

The Devils are not afraid to hire a coach they have already fired. If the club believes he is the right man for the job, the job is his. For example, Jacques Lemaire coached the Devils three different times. Lemaire was known as one of the NHL's smartest players when he skated for the Montreal Canadiens in the 1960s and 1970s. In the 1990s, he used his knowledge to help the Devils win their first Stanley Cup. During his next two stints with New Jersey, Lemaire helped build a team that went on to accomplish great things—but under different coaches.

ONE GREAT DAY

Many fans believe that New Jersey's greatest moment came a few minutes after losing a third straight playoff game to the Philadelphia Flyers in the spring of 2000. The Devils walked off the ice knowing they had dug themselves a deep hole. They were now behind three games to one in the Eastern Conference Finals. No team had ever won the conference finals after losing three games in a row.

Larry Robinson had been named coach of the Devils with only eight games left in the regular season. The players were still learning his style. Up until this moment, they knew him to be a serious, quiet man. It turned out they didn't know him at all. Robinson came into the dressing room with fire in his eyes after the loss to the Flyers. "You guys tried it your way for a while," he screamed. "Now I'm telling you what to do and you'll do it!"

Robinson told the Devils that they had been playing selfish hockey. Each player was trying to be a hero, instead of playing together as a

Larry Robinson and Ken Daneyko share a laugh after both had retired. Things were a bit more tense between the two during the 2000 playoffs.

team. Robinson was furious with two players in particular, Scott Stevens and Ken Daneyko. This stunned the rest of the Devils. Stevens and Daneyko were two of the club's leaders on the ice.

"Individuals win awards— teams win championships," Robinson explained. "We can be the first team to make history. No other team has come back from three-to-one. It's a challenge we should accept."

The Devils were inspired by Robinson's words and began playing together on offense and defense. The Flyers did not know how to respond. New Jersey won the next three games. From there, the Devils were unstoppable. In the Stanley Cup Finals, they beat the Dallas Stars in six games to win the championship.

LEGEND HAS IT

WHO WAS THE MOST NERVOUS PERSON DURING THE 2003 STANLEY CUP FINALS?

LEGEND HAS IT that Carol Niedermayer was. One son, Scott, played for the Devils. Another, Rob, played for the Anaheim Ducks. So many reporters tried to interview her that the Devils

had to set up a press conference. Carol admitted that she was rooting for the Ducks. Scott had already won two championships with the Devils, so it would be nice for Rob to get one. Both of her sons played well, but the Devils *prevailed.* Four years later, the Niedermayer brothers made things easier on their mom. Scott had joined Anaheim. He and Rob were on the ice together when the Ducks won the Stanley Cup in 2007.

ABOVE: Scott Niedermayer offers words of encouragement to Rob after the 2003 Stanley Cup Finals.

WHO GAVE THE MOST FAMOUS AUTOGRAPHS IN TEAM HISTORY?

LEGEND HAS IT that Don Cherry did. Cherry coached the Boston Bruins to four first-place finishes and was very popular with fans in the New England area. However, he was not popular with his boss, Harry Sinden, and was fired after five seasons. The Colorado Rockies snapped him up in 1979. On their first visit to Boston, the Rockies scored a rare victory. With one minute left, Cherry called timeout. He used the break to sign autographs for his cheering fans in the Boston Garden—while Sinden and the team's owners got boiling mad!

WHICH "DEVIL DAD" HAD THE COOLEST JOB?

LEGEND HAS IT that Martin Brodeur's father did. Denis Brodeur was the official team photographer for the Montreal Canadiens, as well as the Montreal Expos baseball team. When young Martin wasn't in school or playing sports, he got to hang out with his dad just inches from the action. He also got to meet lots of baseball and hockey stars. It was Brodeur's close-up view of pro hockey as a boy that gave him a great knowledge of the game—knowledge he put to work during more than two decades as the star of the Devils.

Devils fans often argue about the biggest "stop" in team history. Mostly, they talk about Martin Brodeur, who has made hundreds of great saves. But more than a few Devils will tell you that the man who made the most important stop wasn't wearing a New Jersey sweater. He was wearing a bus driver's uniform. Toward the end of the 2002–03 season, the Devils traded for Grant Marshall. He was so new that one day the team bus left for a game without him—and no one noticed! This wasn't just any game. It was the last game in New Jersey's playoff series with the Tampa Bay Lightning.

When Marshall saw the bus roaring away, he grabbed his bags and ran after it. He chased it up a hill and down a street before the driver spotted him in the mirror and stopped to let him on. That night, the Devils and Lightning played three overtime periods. As the game wore on, Marshall wondered what it would be like to score the winning goal. He pictured himself at the bottom of a pile of happy teammates. "I was really hoping to get the puck and

Grant Marshall screams with joy as his teammates congratulate him after his game-winning goal.

get the goal for the guys," he remembers, "and have them cheering and going crazy."

In the third overtime, Marshall saw his chance. The Devils set up a play for Scott Niedermayer to blast a shot at the Lightning goal. Marshall skated in front of the net to block the view of goalie John Grahame. The Tampa Bay netminder stopped the puck, but it dribbled right onto Marshall's stick. He whacked a backhand into the net to win the game and the series. With help from their newest teammate, the Devils went on to win the Stanley Cup.

TEAM SPIRIT

When a team wins the Stanley Cup, a big parade usually follows. The players ride in cars or on floats through the middle of the city. The fans cheer them from the sidewalks. The three times the Devils won the Stanley Cup, this wasn't possible. They played in an arena that was located in the middle of a swamp. They did not "belong" to any one city.

The team's solution was to drive around the parking lot of their arena. Fans got there early and started their own tailgating parties. The players were able to spend time with the fans. Everyone had fun.

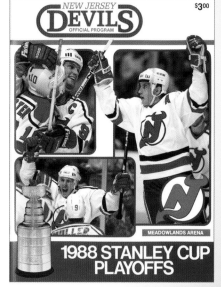

Now the Devils play in the city of Newark. Their next victory celebration probably will go down Broad Street and Market Street, two of the city's major roads. The fans will stand and cheer as loud as they can. Of course, they will never forget those first "parking lot parades."

LEFT: The Devils pose for a picture during their parking lot parade in 2003.
ABOVE: This team program celebrated the team's first trip to the playoffs.

TIMELINE

The hockey season is played from October through June. That means each season takes place at the end of one year and the beginning of the next. In this timeline, the accomplishments of the Scouts, Rockies, and Devils are shown by season …

1976–77
The Scouts move to Colorado and become the Rockies.

1982–83
The Devils play their first season in New Jersey.

1974–75
The team joins the NHL as the Kansas City Scouts.

1987–88
The Devils have their first winning season.

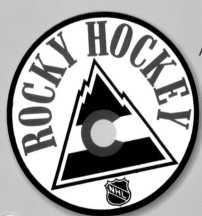

A sticker from the team's years in Colorado.

John MacLean starred for the Devils after their move to New Jersey.

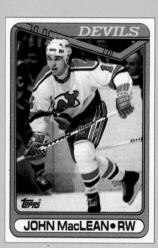

JOHN MacLEAN • RW

John Madden played a key role in 2000 and 2003.

Zach Parise

1994–95
Claude Lemieux leads the Devils to their first Stanley Cup.

2002–03
The team wins its third Stanley Cup.

2011–12
Ilya Kovalchuk and Zach Parise lead the Devils to the Stanley Cup Finals.

1999–2000
The Devils win their second championship.

2003–04
Scott Niedermayer wins the Norris Trophy.

2006–07
Martin Brodeur leads the NHL with 12 shutouts.

Patrik Elias scores during the 2000 Stanley Cup Finals.

FUN FACTS

BREAKING BARRIERS

Scott Gomez was the NHL's first Latino player. He was an *agile* and clever skater who could thread passes through the smallest openings. Gomez led the Devils with 51 assists as a rookie.

FATHER FIGURE

In 2013, the Devils drafted a player with a very famous dad, Anthony Brodeur. His father, Martin, could not have been more proud. He got to announce the team's selection to the crowd assembled at the Devils' home arena.

FINAL TOUCH

During the 1999–2000 season, Martin Brodeur became the first goalie to "score" a game-winning goal. With the score tied 2–2, the Philadelphia Flyers shot the puck into their own net by mistake. Since Brodeur was the last Devil to touch the puck, he got credit for the goal.

ABOVE: Scott Gomez
RIGHT: Mike Rupp

DREAM SEASON

The 2002–03 season was like a dream for **rookie** Mike Rupp. In the first game of his career, he scored two goals. In the final game of the season, he scored the goal that won the Stanley Cup for the Devils.

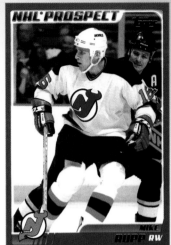

LITTLE BIG MAN

At 5′ 7″, Brian Gionta was one of the smallest players in team history. Even so, he put up one of the Devils' biggest numbers—a team-record 48 goals in 2005–06.

HEY, NO ICING!

For goalie Bob Sauve's final NHL game, the Devils decided to play a practical joke. They stuffed cupcakes into his skates. Sauve played a great game and didn't notice the squishy stuff around his feet until he took his skates off. He still laughs about it. "My feet were completely covered with chocolate!" Sauve says.

LUCKY SEVEN

Most goalies would have been ashamed to allow six goals in their first NHL start. Not Sean Burke. New Jersey's 21-year-old rookie had a big smile on his face when the final siren sounded. His teammates had scored seven times for a 7–6 victory.

TALKING HOCKEY

"To this day, when I think about that game, the plot seems so unreal. It reminds me of a storybook."

▶ **SEAN BURKE,** *on the amazing comeback that sent the team to the playoffs in 1988*

"I'm a firm believer that a big hit could change the **momentum** in a game, just like a big goal could."

▶ **SCOTT STEVENS,** *on his reputation for delivering crunching body checks*

"I was demanding of myself and my teammates. I was willing to do whatever it took to win."

▶ **CLAUDE LEMIEUX,** *on how he approached the playoffs*

"I'm proud to say that not only hockey players followed me. The door opened for people in every profession."

▶ **SLAVA FETISOV**, *on what it meant to be one of the first Russian stars to play pro hockey in the U.S.*

"They appreciate what I stood for as a blue-collar, lunch-pail guy, and how much I loved New Jersey."

▶ **KEN DANEYKO**, *on why he is still a favorite with Devils fans*

"You don't get famous by being a Devil. You get recognized for being part of a winning team."

▶ **MARTIN BRODEUR**, *on being a hockey celebrity in New Jersey*

"Playoffs are the best time of the year. Everything's a challenge, every game means so much."

▶ **COLIN WHITE**, *on the thrill of playing for the Stanley Cup*

LEFT: Sean Burke
ABOVE: Slava Fetisov

GREAT DEBATES

People who root for the Devils love to compare their favorite moments, teams, and players. Some debates have been going on for years! How would you settle these classic hockey arguments?

MARTIN BRODEUR IS WITHOUT A DOUBT THE BEST PLAYER IN TEAM HISTORY ...

... because he was at the top of his game for more than 20 seasons. What made Brodeur so good for so long was that he studied the great scorers. He knew what they would do before they knew themselves. When it looked as if a shooter had Brodeur at his mercy, it was often the other way around—opponents could not guess what his next move would be.

SCOTT STEVENS WAS THE GREATEST DEVIL OF THEM ALL ...

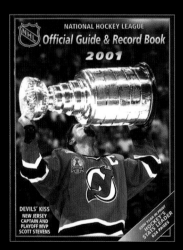

NATIONAL HOCKEY LEAGUE
NHL Official Guide & Record Book
2001

DEVILS' KISS
NEW JERSEY
CAPTAIN AND
PLAYOFF MVP
SCOTT STEVENS

... because without him, Brodeur would have had to stop a lot more shots. It has been said many times that a goalie is only as good as the defensemen in front of him. Stevens (LEFT) was big, fast, and smart. He could steal a pass, block a shot, or knock an opponent off his skates with a crushing body check. When Stevens was in the game, the Devils never had to worry about his half of the ice.

THE NEUTRAL ZONE TRAP STARTED BY THE DEVILS CHANGED HOCKEY FOR THE BETTER . . .

. . . because it gave an advantage to teams that played smart defense. Coach Jacques Lemaire (RIGHT) developed the trap to keep teams from igniting their offense in the center-ice area between the blue lines. The Devils would force the puck to one of the sideboards, and then the forwards and defensemen would work together to block opponents and force a bad pass. Without the trap, New Jersey might never have won a Stanley Cup.

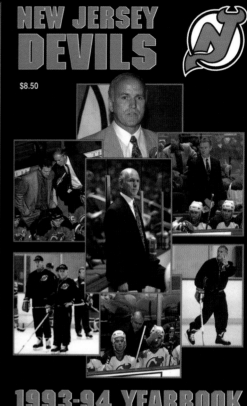

NEW JERSEY
DEVILS

$8.50

1993-94 YEARBOOK

THIS STRATEGY WAS BAD FOR HOCKEY . . .

. . . because it made games boring. Fans pay to see fast, exciting players, and the trap took these stars out of the game. The NHL came to this conclusion in 2005. The league told officials to call penalties any time a player was *obstructed*. The NHL also legalized long passes that crossed two lines, so teams could make use of their fastest skaters. If the trap changed hockey for the better, why was it taken out of the game?

FOR THE RECORD

The great Devils teams and players have left their marks on the record books. These are the "best of the best" …

Martin Brodeur

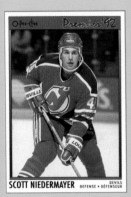

Scott Niedermayer

DEVILS AWARD WINNERS

CALDER TROPHY
TOP ROOKIE

Martin Brodeur	1993–94
Scott Gomez	1999–00

CONN SMYTHE TROPHY
MVP DURING PLAYOFFS

Claude Lemieux	1994–95
Scott Stevens	1999–00

JAMES NORRIS MEMORIAL TROPHY
TOP DEFENSEMAN

Scott Niedermayer	2003–04

FRANK J. SELKE TROPHY
TOP DEFENSIVE FORWARD

John Madden	2000–01

VEZINA TROPHY
TOP GOALTENDER

Martin Brodeur	2002–03
Martin Brodeur	2003–04
Martin Brodeur	2006–07
Martin Brodeur	2007–08

JACK ADAMS AWARD
COACH OF THE YEAR

Jacques Lemaire	1993–94

Devils fans wore this pin after the team moved to New Jersey.

DEVILS ACHIEVEMENTS

ACHIEVEMENT	YEAR
Stanley Cup Champions	1994–95
Stanley Cup Champions	1999–00
Stanley Cup Finalists	2000–01
Stanley Cup Champions	2002–03
Stanley Cup Finalists	2011–12

ABOVE: Ken Daneyko spent his entire playing career with the Devils. After he retired, he became an announcer for the team.
LEFT: Bruce Driver leads the celebration after New Jersey's first championship in 1995.

PINPOINTS

T he history of a hockey team is made up of many smaller stories. These stories take place all over the map—not just in the city a team calls "home." Match the pushpins on these maps to the **TEAM FACTS**, and you will begin to see the story of the Devils unfold!

TEAM FACTS

1   Newark, New Jersey—*The Devils have played here since 2007.*

2   Cloquet, Minnesota—*Jamie Langenbrunner was born here.*

3   Winchester, Massachusetts—*Jay Pandolfo was born here.*

4   Denver, Colorado—*The team moved here from Kansas City in 1976.*

5   Anchorage, Alaska—*Scott Gomez was born here.*

6   Montreal, Quebec—*Martin Brodeur was born here.*

7   Windsor, Ontario—*Ken Daneyko was born here.*

8   Oshawa, Ontario—*John MacLean was born here.*

9   Moose Jaw, Saskatchewan—*Chico Resch was born here.*

10   Vancouver, British Columbia—*Barry Beck was born here.*

11   Jihlava, Czech Republic—*Bobby Holik was born here.*

12   Moscow, Russia—*Sergei Brylin was born here.*

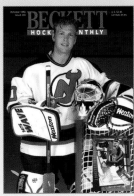

Martin Brodeur

GLOSSARY

🏒 HOCKEY WORDS
🧠 VOCABULARY WORDS

🧠 *AGILE*—Quick and graceful.

🏒 **ALL-STAR GAME**—The annual game that features the best players from the NHL.

🧠 *ARCH-RIVAL*—A team's most competitive opponent.

🏒 **ASSISTS**—Passes that lead to a goal.

🧠 *CENTURY*—A period of 100 years.

🏒 **CHECKS**—Body blows that stop an opponent from advancing with the puck.

🧠 *CLUTCH*—Performing well under pressure.

🏒 **CONFERENCE**—A large group of teams. There are two conferences in the NHL, and each season each conference sends a team to the Stanley Cup Finals.

🏒 **CREASE**—The area in front of the goal, between the two red circles in the defensive end.

🧠 *DECADE*—A period of 10 years; also specific periods, such as the 1950s.

🏒 **DRAFT**—The annual meeting during which NHL teams pick the top high school, college, and international players.

🧠 *ERA*—A period of time in history.

🧠 *FORMULA*—A set way of doing something.

🧠 *LABORED*—Worked hard.

🧠 *LOGO*—A symbol or design that represents a company or team.

🏒 **MAJOR-LEAGUE**—The highest level of professional sports.

🧠 *MOMENTUM*—Strength or force built up during an event.

🏒 **MOST VALUABLE PLAYER (MVP)**—The award given each year to the league's best player; also given to the best player in the playoffs and All-Star Game.

🏒 **NATIONAL HOCKEY LEAGUE (NHL)**—The professional league that has been operating since 1917.

🧠 *OBSTRUCTED*—Blocked from moving forward.

🧠 *OLYMPICS*—An international summer or winter sports competition held every four years.

🏒 **OVERTIME**—An extra period played when a game is tied after three periods. In the NHL playoffs, teams continue to play overtime periods until a goal is scored.

🏒 **PENALTY-KILLER**—A player who takes the ice when his team is short-handed.

🏒 **PLAYOFFS**—The games played after the season to determine the league champion.

🏒 **POSTSEASON**—Another term for playoffs.

🏒 **POWER PLAY**—A game situation in which one team has at least one extra skater on the ice. A power play occurs when a player commits a penalty and is sent to the penalty box.

🧠 *PREVAILED*—Proved to be more successful or powerful.

🏒 **PROFESSIONAL**—A player or team that plays a sport for money.

🏒 **ROOKIE**—A player in his first year.

🏒 **ROSTER**—The list of a team's active players.

🏒 **SHUTOUTS**—Games in which a team doesn't score a goal.

🏒 **STANLEY CUP FINALS**—The final playoff series that determines the winner of the Stanley Cup, which is the trophy presented to the NHL champion.

🏒 **VETERANS**—Players with great experience.

🏒 **WORLD HOCKEY ASSOCIATION (WHA)**—The league that operated from 1972 to 1979.

LINE CHANGE

TEAM SPIRIT introduces a great way to stay up to date with your team! Visit our *LINE CHANGE* link and get connected to the latest and greatest updates. *LINE CHANGE* serves as a young reader's ticket to an exclusive web page—with more stories, fun facts, team records, and photos of the Devils. Content is updated during and after each season. The *LINE CHANGE* feature also enables readers to send comments and letters to the author! Log onto:

www.norwoodhousepress.com/library.aspx

and click on the tab: **TEAM SPIRIT** to access *LINE CHANGE*.

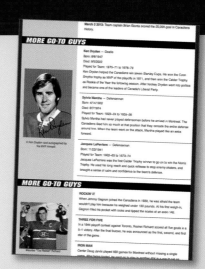

Read all the books in the series to learn more about professional sports. For a complete listing of the baseball, basketball, football, and hockey teams in the **TEAM SPIRIT** series, visit our website at:

www.norwoodhousepress.com/library.aspx

ON THE ROAD

NEW JERSEY DEVILS
165 Mulberry Street
Newark, New Jersey 07102
(973) 757-6100
http://devils.nhl.com

HOCKEY HALL OF FAME
Brookfield Place
30 Yonge Street
Toronto, Ontario, Canada M5E 1X8
(416) 360-7765
http://www.hhof.com

ON THE BOOKSHELF

To learn more about the sport of hockey, look for these books at your library or bookstore:

- Cameron, Steve. *Hockey Hall of Fame Treasures.* Richmond Hill, Ontario, Canada: Firefly Books, 2011.

- MacDonald, James. *Hockey Skills: How to Play Like a Pro.* Berkeley Heights, New Jersey: Enslow Elementary, 2009.

- Keltie, Thomas. *Inside Hockey! The legends, facts, and feats that made the game.* Toronto, Ontario, Canada: Maple Tree Press, 2008.

INDEX

PAGE NUMBERS IN **BOLD** REFER TO ILLUSTRATIONS.

THE TEAM

MARK STEWART has written over 200 books for kids—and more than a dozen books on hockey, including a history of the Stanley Cup and an authorized biography of goalie Martin Brodeur. He grew up in New York City during the 1960s rooting for the Rangers, but has gotten to know a couple of New Jersey Devils, so he roots for a shootout when these teams play each other. Mark comes from a family of writers. His grandfather was Sunday Editor of *The New York Times*, and his mother was Articles Editor of *Ladies' Home Journal* and *McCall's*. Mark has profiled hundreds of athletes over the past 25 years. He has also written several books about his native New York and New Jersey, his home today. Mark is a graduate of Duke University, with a degree in history. He lives and works in a home overlooking Sandy Hook, New Jersey. You can contact Mark through the Norwood House Press website.

DENIS GIBBONS is a writer and editor with *The Hockey News* and a former newsletter editor of the Toronto-based Society for International Hockey Research (SIHR). He was a contributing writer to the publication *Kings of the Ice: A History of World Hockey* and has worked as chief hockey researcher at five Winter Olympics for the ABC, CBS, and NBC television networks. Denis also has worked as a researcher for the FOX Sports Network during the Stanley Cup playoffs. He resides in Burlington, Ontario, Canada with his wife Chris.

43